MAKE~UP FOR BRUNETTES

SUSI ROGOL

Villard Books   New York   1984

Also by Susi Rogol

Make-up for Blondes
Make-up for Redheads
Make-up for Blacks

Copyright © 1984 by Marshall Editions Ltd

Library of Congress Catalog Card Number: 84-40032
ISBN: 0-394-72616-2

Typeset by MS Filmsetting Ltd, Frome, Somerset, England
Reproduced by Gilchrist Bros Ltd, Leeds, England
Printed and bound in Belgium by Brepols SA

9 8 7 6 5 4 3 2
First Edition

Editor
Rosanne Hooper

Art Director
John Bigg

Design
Katrina Dallamore and Sharon Lovett

Text editor
Gwen Rigby

Photography   **Illustrations**
Bill Ling   Liz Gill

Models
Beverly (Askews) cover, p 19
Melanie Wilson (Models One) pp 7, 13
Harriet Close (Laraine Ashton) pp 21, 48–51
Gail Elliot (Models One) pp 33, 37, 60, 61
Virginie (Take 2) pp 44–47
Annagret (Penny) pp 52–55
Maureen Thompson (Top Models) pp 56–9

Make-up artists
Yvonne Gold, Mary Greenwell, Cheryl Phelps,
Sara Raeburn

Hair stylists
Derek Morris (Bookings), Paul Yacamino (Neville
Daniel), Elliot (Michaeljohn), Mario (Michaeljohn)

Jewelry   **Evening Clothes**
Monet   Wayne Clark

Contents

Introduction

Once upon a time, not so very long ago, those born beautiful were regarded as the lucky ones, while their "Plain Jane" sisters just stayed that way. Attitudes have changed, as have the ideals of beauty. Today the classical, perfectly formed face often goes unnoticed alongside the chic good-looks of a woman who has developed her own sense of style and individuality. Right now, in the educated 80s, we are living with an "anything-goes" acceptance of beauty and fashion. Every woman has the opportunity to take advantage of the wealth of skin care, colour cosmetic and hair products readily available, in order to create her own special look.

YOUR HAIR

Let's start with your hair; your crowning glory.

Whatever its length, its style, its type, you will want it to look great all day, every day. Brunettes come in many shades, from the lightest golden brown, through the mid-tones, to the deepest and darkest bitter-chocolate brown that is often mistaken for black. In between there is a multitude of colours, some warm and vibrant, others soft and subtle.

Lighter brunettes have quite a lot of blonde pigmentation in their hair, and exposure to the sun or a lemon juice rinse will help produce the natural, fair highlights. Darker shades of brown usually contain some red, and when treated with a henna compound, they sparkle with a fiery glow.

But whatever your shade, it is important to keep your hair in good shape, well looked after and expertly cut to a manageable style, which flatters your face.

Greasy hair, a common problem with dark brunettes, needs frequent washing with a mild, non-detergent shampoo. It should be brushed only when necessary, to avoid stimulating the already over-active sebaceous glands. Diet, too, can help control oil production, so avoid fatty or highly spiced foods and an excess of tea and coffee.

Dry hair, on the other hand, is often caused by external factors; too much heat (the sun, electric rollers, tongs and dryers), bleaching, perming, tinting or straightening. Condition it well and often.

Most shades of brown hair are enhanced by highlights or lowlights; the paler shades with streaks of honey, wheat, cream and ash; the darker ones with shimmering strands of chestnut, rich auburn and copper. As an alternative to all-over lights, try really pale colours on the front half of the head for a young, fun and quite different look. Remember, though, that highlights need retouching only every four to five months, while permanent tints require more maintenance.

Regular once-a-month visits to the hairdresser may be necessary to cope with new hair growth. Semi-permanent rinses, designed to brighten your natural colour, are quite effective, and the results last for approximately four weeks.

Headlines

If your hair looks a mess—if it is too greasy, too dry, badly coloured or roughly cut—no matter how well you are made-up or how beautifully dressed, you simply will not look, or feel, great. Hair is one of the most important beauty-makers and is one that gets noticed, so time and trouble invested on your tresses will pay dividends. If you find a style that suits your face, is versatile and easy to manage, then your hair will never let you down nor spoil your special image.

Take note ...

● A good cut is the best investment you can make. Find a hairdresser who is an expert with scissors and never try to cut your hair yourself.

● Have your hair cut and shaped regularly, even if you are planning a longer length. Hair does not grow uniformly and goes through untidy phases, when its shape is lost.

Perming

It is best to consult an expert before going ahead with a capful of curls. Perming lifts colour, so you will have to wait the appropriate time between a perm and a colour retouch. Think carefully before opting for a perm or any new style and be sure that it suits you and that it you will be able to cope with it at home. Be particularly wary of passing trends for crazy colours or stiffly gelled spikes—they raise a lot of laughs and add years to anyone over twenty.

Hair sprays

If you use hair spray, it is especially important to keep your hair in tip-top condition. After-shampoo protein rinses keep the hair tangle-free and full of bounce and shine. Try using hair sprays in a new way. Spray the hair lightly first, then arrange it with your fingertips. A final layer of lacquer after arranging the hair often gives it a stiff, unnatural and old-fashioned look.

STYLES TO SUIT YOUR FACE SHAPE

The round face

Long hair is fine if you keep the style soft to frame the face and reshape the outline. Don't wear a full fringe, it will shorten the face. Short crops look great if kept casual and are best brushed forward in gentle wisps.

The heart-shaped face

This face shape can carry most styles well but looks especially stunning in high-fashion numbers, like the short, sharp bob. Equally successful are the soft, puffy styles, with fullness behind the ears and thick, wavy fringes.

The long face

If the forehead is left uncovered, long faces look longer still. A heavy fringe and fullness above the ears adds balance and plays up the eyes. An umbrella cut works wonders, too, cropped short at the back but left long and full at the sides.

The square face

One of the strongest face shapes and stylish in its own right, the square face can be softened with a mass of loose curls at the neck. Or it can be accentuated with the hair scraped up on top in a curly knot, pinned and fluffed out, forties style, into a bunch of waves.

Your skin type

Although no two skins are exactly the same, most have characteristics which, for ease of classification, enable them to be grouped according to type—dry, greasy, normal, combination and sensitive. Once you know and understand each group, it is easier to analyze your own skin and its problems and to choose the skin care and cosmetics best suited to your individual needs.

Take note ...
● Study your face carefully and identify your own skin type. Watch out for any changes in the condition of your skin.

● Remember that dry, thirsty skin ages prematurely. It quickly loses its smoothness and elasticity, so keep it well moisturized.

DRY SKIN
Although not so common among dark-haired, darker-skinned brunettes, dry skin is often found with a fair complexion. It needs a lot of loving attention and suffers badly in extreme temperatures. It feels taut after washing and has a tendency toward flakiness, small broken veins and reddish patches. Dry skin also ages prematurely and appears to be more wrinkle-prone than other types because of its lack of natural elasticity; even the finest lines seem to be etched deeply. Constant protection is highly important, and products used must be mild and gentle in their formulation but also rich and soothing.

GREASY SKIN
Oily skin is the result of over-active sebaceous glands producing an excess of sebum, which flows to the surface of the skin through the pores. When the pores become blocked, they enlarge and become a breeding ground for spots, blackheads and possibly acne. Scrupulous cleansing is as vital as the exclusion of fatty foods from your diet. A regular once-a-week steam treatment will help unclog the pores and draw out the plugs of sebum that turn into blackheads. These must be removed and, after steaming, should be squeezed out between two clean tissues. Blot the area afterwards with an antiseptic cotton ball.

NORMAL SKIN

The classification of normal skin is really quite strange, simply because, as a skin type, it is something of a rarity and, therefore, not the norm at all. Those very few, very lucky people who can claim to have perfectly balanced skin will enjoy one which is neither dry nor greasy, that looks healthy and glowing, is evenly coloured and textured and never acneic or veined. This skin type is not affected by changes of temperature or diet, but still needs sensible and gentle care to keep it in its enviably perfect condition. A regular beauty regime with well-balanced products should do the trick.

SENSITIVE SKIN

Always difficult, sensitive skin is usually dry but can sometimes be greasy. It flares up easily, develops allergies to foods and cosmetic products. It reddens or pales when faced with emotional upsets and hormonal changes. Other signs of sensitive skin are cuperos (small, red, broken veins), sore patches and itchy spots. Those with severe problems should consult their doctor and ask for a referral to a dermatologist for specialized advice. Others should always use skin care and cosmetic products formulated for sensitive skins and avoid the foods that produce a reaction.

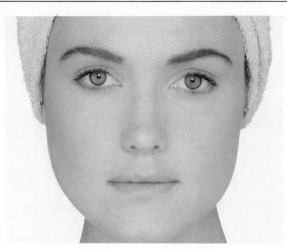

COMBINATION SKIN

Most of us have combination skin, which is part dry, especially on the cheeks, with grease-prone patches on the forehead, nose and chin. If the difference between the two is great, treat each part of the face accordingly: the dry areas as for dry skin, with suitably formulated, mild and gentle products; the center panel as for greasy skin, with astringent toners and less-rich moisturizers.

Face facts

If beauty is skin deep, it stands to reason that skin care is by far the most important aspect of beauty. No amount of make-up, however skilfully applied, can hide the damage caused by neglect. If you follow a sensible beauty regime and a healthy diet and understand your skin and its needs, you will have the reassurance that you are doing the best for your looks now, and in the future. Remember, you have only one face, and that face has to last you a lifetime ... so look after it.

Take note ...
- Your skin care routine must be regular—morning and night, seven days a week.
- However tired you are, never go to bed without removing every trace of make-up.

- Choose products made for your skin type, particularly if you have sensitive skin, acne or allergies.
- Sun, cold weather and central heating dry out the skin, so use protective creams.

SKIN CARE PRODUCTS

Cleansers, 1
Cream or milky cleansers should be massaged into the face and neck. Some are removed with tissues, others with water. The new foaming cleansers and soaps that froth up on the face are rinsed off.

Toners, 2
These are designed to remove the last traces of dirt and cleanser, to refresh and refine the skin and to tighten pores. Always use one designed for your skin type—the stronger, astringent toners are far too harsh for non-oily faces.

Moisturizers, 3
They nourish the skin and replace valuable fluids that are lost in the course of a day. Most are quickly absorbed and leave a non-greasy,

protective film. The tinted kinds give a healthy, outdoor glow and can be worn alone or under foundation.

Night creams, 4
These extra-rich creams contain nutrients to feed the face while you sleep. They help smooth away fine lines and wrinkles and their use becomes vital as the skin matures. Young skins can use a moisturizer at night.

Eye make-up removers, 5
There are oils, gels and saturated pads, designed to remove eye make-up, particularly waterproof types. Wipe gently over the eye area—never pull or drag at delicate skin—and remove with a damp cotton ball.

THE ROUTINE

Every morning

Splash the face with cold water for a refreshing "wake-up" for the skin. Cleanse thoroughly with a facial bar, foaming cleanser or light, fluid cream cleanser. Remove with tissue, cotton ball or water and pat the face dry. Pour your toner on a clean cotton ball and pat all over the face in upward and outward movements. Give those areas prone to oiliness—the cheeks on each side of the nostrils, the chin, the forehead—an extra pat or two. Apply a fine film of moisturizer over the entire face and throat. Wait a few minutes before applying any make-up.

Every night

Cleanse the face with great care; you must remove every trace of make-up, grease and the tiny particles of dirt and grit that find their way on to your face during the day. Apply your cleanser over the whole face and neck and remove it with tissue, cotton ball or water, depending on the cleanser type. Wipe over the face again with a damp cotton ball, and if it does not come away clean, repeat the cleansing process. Now, take off your eye make-up. Use a damp cotton ball to remove both cleanser and make-up, and be gentle, to avoid causing irritation to the eyes or pulling at the sensitive surrounding tissue. Go over the lashes carefully, with a cotton swab dampened with remover, until all mascara has vanished. Tone the face well, and wipe over the eyelids to remove any oily residue.

Apply a fine film of moisturizer—night cream if your skin is dry or mature—and massage lightly into the skin in small, semi-circular, up and outward movements. Avoid an excess of cream—your face could puff up as a result.

Always try to get a good night's sleep.

11

The beauty boosters

One of the best and quickest ways to give your skin an instant beauty booster is with a face mask. Most are designed to deep cleanse, others to tighten pores or slough off dead skin cells, and all of them leave the skin soft, smooth and glowing. There is a wide variety of masks to choose from that are designed for specific skin types or to cope with certain problems, but just as successful are the ones you can conjure up at home, using fresh fruit, vegetables and dairy products.

Take note ...
- Masks should always be used on a clean face.
- Only use a mask for your own skin type.
- The benefits of a mask are increased if the skin is slightly warm. After cleansing, press a hot washcloth lightly over the whole face.
- Avoid the eyes and ensure you cover the face evenly, especially open pore areas.
- Sit or lie down and relax while your mask is doing its job. Place dampened tea bags or cotton balls on the eyes to help soothe away signs of tiredness.

TYPES OF MASKS
Cleansing masks are the most common type and often contain clay, which absorbs impurities, helps remove blackheads and tightens the pores. Most of them are thick and creamy and dry out while they are working. Remove with lukewarm water and splash the face with cold water or a mild toning lotion. The skin is left smooth and youthful-looking and fine lines are temporarily erased.

Exfoliating masks are especially good for more mature skins for they help remove the dead surface cells and stimulate the formation of new ones. The chemical types work by dissolving the dead cells, and the others by gentle abrasion. Be careful to remove every trace of the mask afterwards or you will find yourself peeling away small patches of it hours later.

Cream masks are the newest breed and are especially good for very dry or sensitive skins and for frequent use. They do not exfoliate, but they do smooth and refine the skin's texture, giving a fresh bloom to the complexion.

Gel masks are often made with herbs, minerals, fruit or vegetables. They are fun to use because they are often brightly coloured and dry to a fine film which can be peeled off in one movement. These are real refreshers and leave the skin glowing with health.

D.I.Y. masks are what Clare Maxwell Hudson, one of the world's leading exponents of natural beauty, recommends. Masks you can mix up or whip together in the kitchen do feed your face, but don't be tempted to eat the remains—some of them can be lethal to the waistline!

Try mashing half a banana with two spoons of cream and a teaspoon of honey. Add a few drops of orange juice if your skin is greasy. Smooth over the face and leave on for 15 minutes.

For spots and problem skins, whip up an egg white, add a crushed garlic clove and a teaspoon each of carrot juice and honey; leave on the face for 10 to 20 minutes.

Don't forget natural yogurt—it's the quickest and easiest pick-me-up for tired skin.

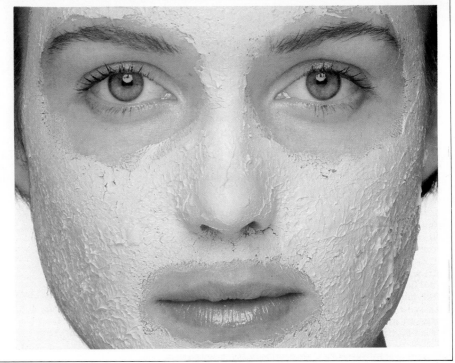

Cool complexions

Get your base right, in texture, colour and application, and you have laid the foundation of a beautiful make-up—a smooth, perfectly toned canvas on which you can then create an ever-changing variety of new and different looks.

Take note ...
- Choose a shade that matches the darkest part of your face or, better still, your neck or breastbone. Avoid shades that are tinged with pink. Never test colours on your wrist or under artificial light.
- If your skin is greasy, look for a water-based foundation.
- Dry skins will benefit from an enriched, oil-based foundation.

- Normal skins can stay with a liquid cream for light, even coverage.
- Never layer your foundation over stale make-up. Your skin will suffer, and the look created will be far from beautiful.
- Those with dark hair and pale skin look perfect in a fragile, ivory-toned foundation, as long as plenty of colour is used to bring a warm blush to the cheeks.

FOUNDATION TYPES

Liquid cream, 1
Coverage: light
Application: fingertips

Stick foundation, 3
Coverage: medium/heavy
Application: with sponge

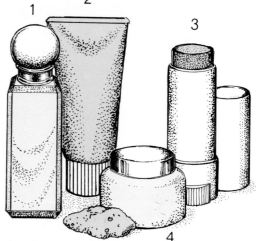

Lotion foundation, 2
Coverage: light
Application: fingertips

Cream foundation, 4
Coverage: medium/heavy
Application: with sponge

APPLICATION

Foundations are designed to give a soft, even, natural glow to the face. The best coverage comes with the use of the right colour and product type for your skin, not from the amount you apply.

Put a little on the back of your hand and then dot it on the nose, on the cheeks, the chin, the temples and between the eyebrows. Always work from the center of the face out, to avoid an accumulation around the hair-line and to ensure even application.

Using the tips of two fingers or a small, clean, dampened sponge, blend foundation from the cheeks out to the ears; from the temples up and out to the hair-line; from between the eyebrows down over the nose; from

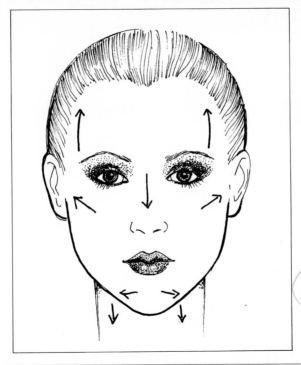

the chin out toward the jaw then downward on to the neck.

Work quickly and carefully, blending all the time, and take special care around the hair-line, on the neck, below the eyes and behind the ears. Always take foundation over the eyelids. Use a concealer stick in the same colour to cover small veins and blemishes. Blend well into surrounding areas.

Once your foundation is complete, blot over the face with a clean, dry tissue. In addition to your favourite cream or liquid foundation, buy at least two other shades, one lighter and one darker, plus a pale-toned concealer in crayon or stick form.

Changing shapes

No woman is totally happy with her looks and most would like to be able to make a few small changes. A bit of know-how and a few magical tricks can reshape and contour the face, correct faults and minimize the problem areas.

Take note ...
● Cleanse, tone and nourish your face; tie back your hair and study yourself in a well-lit mirror. Pinpoint any faults that need some correction. Remember, though, that a single dimple or a sprinkling of freckles can be most attractive and give the face an appealing individuality.

● Never overdo it when reshaping the features or bone structure. You can run the risk of emphasizing the very point you are trying to conceal.
● Always carry your base foundation over the neck and throat and behind the ears, then blend well. Nothing looks worse than bands of colour or a face two shades lighter than the neck.

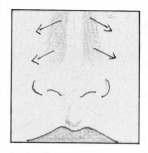 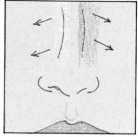

To slim down a wide nose
After applying your foundation, but always before powdering, blend a darker foundation down each side of the nose, starting at the bridge, and smoothing slightly outward. Use a soft, flat brush, your fingertip or a wedge-shaped piece of sponge and blend in well.

To straighten a crooked nose
A crooked nose simply needs balancing to make it look smooth and straight. Work out exactly where the fault lies and make your main adjustment on the opposite side. Use a darker foundation on the problem side, a lighter shade opposite.

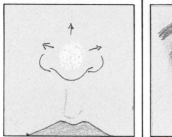

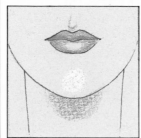

To turn up a drooped nose
The impression of a pretty tilted nose can be achieved by using a very light foundation or a dot of concealer stick right on the tip of the nose, just above the nostrils. Be sparing when applying highlighter and blend well—a droopy nose is better than a white blob.

Under-eye shadows
Dark shadows and bags can often be caused by lack of sleep, stress and bad eating habits. Consult a doctor if the problem is severe. Soothe puffiness with an eye mask (squeezed-out tea bags are excellent) and lighten the shadows with a pale concealer stick, blended well.

To correct a receding chin
Always stand straight and with shoulders back; many chins that appear to recede are the result of bad posture. Apply a circle of pale foundation on the pad of the chin and blend well. Add a darker colour in a soft U-shape under the chin and on the center of the throat.

To soften a heavy jaw
Use a dark foundation or contouring cream along the jawline; deeper just below the cheeks, lighter to the side of the chin. Blend well in all directions, taking great care to smooth colour lightly toward the neck. Add a touch of lighter tone at the tip of the chin and pat over the face.

17

Setting your make-up

Powder does two things. Firstly, it sets your make-up perfectly and gives a smooth, even finish to the complexion. Secondly, it helps prevent shine-through on the areas most prone to oiliness: the center panel of the face and the forehead. Loose powder is by far the best (pressed versions tend to cake and streak), and if it is applied correctly, your make-up should stay fresh and pretty-looking throughout the longest day and into the evening.

Take note ...
● Find a fine, loose powder, preferably fragrance-free. Some of the perfumed types smell stale after a few hours.

● Opt for translucent powder; it looks soft and natural, unlike some tinted ones which grey on the face or colour too brightly.

Special effects
It is worth experimenting with special-effect powders, which are designed to correct problems of coloration. A pale green helps to tone down a pink complexion, while mauve neutralizes very strong colouring. Always apply these carefully and lightly and never retouch. Don't forget shimmer powders. They can look terrific on young skin or whisked over a golden tan. For the evening, try a sparkling glitter-powder, on the shoulders, collar-bones and high on the cheeks, over blusher. A tiny dab of gold powder on the earlobe helps to set off a pretty earring.

APPLICATION
Before applying powder, make sure that your foundation is well blended around the hair-line, over the throat and behind the ears and that there are no lines where concealers have been used. Blot the face lightly with a tissue, especially over the forehead, nose and chin. Pick up powder on the puff and press it firmly on the face and neck, one area at a time. Don't try to smooth it on by massaging the puff over the face. Now, using a soft, thick powder brush, whisk away the surplus, with a downward movement to stop powder getting caught in the fine facial hairs.

Adding a blush

Blushers probably do more for a face than any other cosmetic product. They can add shape and definition and also highlight a good feature; they can give the complexion a wonderfully warm, youthful glow; they can make the eyes come alive.

Take note ...
● Blushers are available in pressed powder, cream or stick form. Go for powder every time, it is easier to apply and gives a really soft finish.
● All brunettes should avoid blue-toned blushers, drab browns and dusty shades. Medium to dark brunettes look best in warm pink or peachy corals, light brunettes in soft pinks and apricots.

● Always use a blusher brush. Most powder blushers come complete with their own, but it is a good idea to invest in a really thick, fluffy one.
● Mature skins look far better in soft shades of matt blusher. Leave the fun, frosted colours to the youngsters.
● Don't put too much blusher on your brush; always tap the brush on the back of your hand to remove any surplus.

1 Slim down the face by applying blusher just below the cheekbone, sweeping it softly up and out toward the center of the ear. Try a pale coral and repeat it beneath the jaw, very lightly, to bring the chin forward.

2 To give the face a warm, sun-kissed glow, use an apricot blusher, with a hint of pink, fluffed over the cheeks and out toward the ears. Continue up to the sides of the eyes and under the outer half of the brows.

3 The prettiest of blushers is wonderfully natural—a soft, mid-pink with a touch of peach. Dab blusher lightly over the whole cheek, above and below the bone, and continue it up in a gentle sweep over the temples.

4 For night-time drama and sophistication, choose a stronger-coloured blusher to tone with your clothes. Try a rich coral with black, cream or the brights, a pink-cinnamon with just about anything else.

Shaping up

Eyebrows give the face its expression, framing the eyes and balancing the features. High, thin arches look hard and unnatural, shaggy curves are heavy and unfeminine. It is worth spending the time to get your eyebrows into good shape—you will see a beautiful difference in your looks.

Take note ...
● Never use a hair-removing product on your eyebrows and never go near them with a razor or electric shaver.
● Buy the sort of tweezers that have slanted or squared-off ends, they are much easier to use than the pointed type. Make sure the grip is firm.

● To try to change your natural eyebrow shape totally is a big mistake. Most eyebrows simply need tidying up and shaping to keep them looking good.
● Even if your eyebrows arch naturally, avoid a perfectly inverted V unless you want to appear in a state of permanent surprise.

Balance
The single most important point to remember when shaping your eyebrows is balance. Thin eyebrows can make a face look flat and drained and will emphasize puffiness around the eyes. Heavy, straight eyebrows will take over the face and detract from the eyes.

WHERE TO START

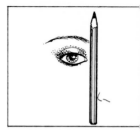

There are a few rules, worth following if you want to do the job properly.

Sit in front of the mirror, take a pencil and hold it so as to make a line from the side of the nostril to the inner corner of the eye and up. Where it touches the eyebrow is your starting point.

WHERE TO FINISH

Now hold the pencil at an angle, from the side of the nostril, past the outer corner of the eye and out. This will give you the ideal point at which the eyebrow should end.

Looking straight ahead, you will find the highest point for the eyebrow—it should be directly above the iris.

GETTING THE SHAPE RIGHT

Before you get busy with the tweezers, clean your face well and wipe your eyebrows with a skin toner to remove every trace of grease. Tie back your hair and study your face in the mirror to decide on the shape that will look right.

Brush the eyebrows upward with a clean mascara brush or soft toothbrush. When shaping them, never pluck from above, always from beneath, and hold the skin taut between your first and second fingers. Hold tweezers firmly in the other hand and grip each hair as close as possible to the root. Use short, quick movements, remove only one hair at a time and always pluck in the direction of hair growth.

First remove any stragglers from between the brows, then tidy the general outline. If your eyebrows are thick and straight, taper them from the center to the outer end. Go slowly and avoid removing big chunks, or your eyebrows will look patchy and demand too much pencilling. Don't cut long hairs with scissors. When you have finished, brush the eyebrows again, wipe them with a mild toner and use a tiny amount of moisturizer to soothe the skin. Do wait a while before applying make-up.

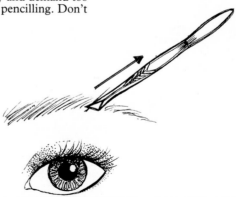

Defining the eyebrows

Eyebrows that are distinctly pencilled or over-shaped can spoil a look and add years to the appearance. Practice a little, on a clean face, using finely sharpened pencils or eyebrow powders; then you can wipe away mistakes and start again until you get the shape and style just right.

Take note ...
● If your eyebrows are very light, have them tinted professionally at a beauty salon or at the hairdresser.
● Remember that eyebrow colouring should not contrast with the hair.
● Pick a fine pencil in a colour to tone with your eyebrows and always keep the point well sharpened.

● If you opt for eyebrow powder, choose one that comes with a slant-tipped brush or buy a brush separately. Squared-off brushes and rounded applicators are difficult to use.
● High arches and solid lines are hard and ugly; too-dark eyebrows are aging.
● Always brush eyebrows up and out before using pencils or powder.

A delicate touch
When using a pencil, always use straight, tiny strokes and follow the direction of natural hair growth. With powder, use the smallest amount by tapping the brush on the back of your hand to remove any surplus. Apply it in short, feathery strokes, to keep the line soft and natural. Remember that defining the eyebrows comes after you have achieved the shape and colour you want and after applying powder and foundation.

When you have the shape, style and degree of fullness right, you will be ready for a full make-up. Define the eyebrows after you have applied foundation and powder but before eyeshadow.

THE EQUIPMENT

Eyebrow pencil

Mascara brush

Slant-ended brush

Sharpener

Eyebrow
powder

APPLICATION

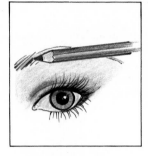

Powder eyebrows lightly with translucent powder and remove any surplus. Then brush with a clean mascara brush.

Apply pencil or powder in short, light, upward strokes. Always start at the inner corner of the eyebrow and work toward the middle. Go carefully and make sure that the pencilled strokes are really fine and follow the natural line of growth.

From the center of the eyebrow to the outer end, use the same feathery strokes, but this time, tipping downward.

Brush eyebrows again with a mascara brush and, for an ultra-soft look, dust over lightly with translucent powder.

Shadow techniques

Making eyes come alive is a real art and, like any good artist, you will need to learn first the exacting techniques of accurate brushwork and careful colour-blending. Invest in the best accessories if you want professional results.

Take note ...
- Eye shadow comes in various forms: pressed powder, loose powder, cream sticks and liquid cream, in both matt and frosted shades. Pressed powder types are the easiest to use, loose powders the most difficult. Cream sticks tend to go into creases after a few hours; liquid types often streak unless applied skilfully.

- Heavy or wrinkled lids look better with matt colour; glitter can be unkind.
- Always apply make-up in good light, daylight if possible.
- Don't be tempted to buy kits with lots of colours if you are only going to use a couple. Go instead for a shadow trio which offers light, medium and deeper tones of the same colour.

SHADOW TYPES

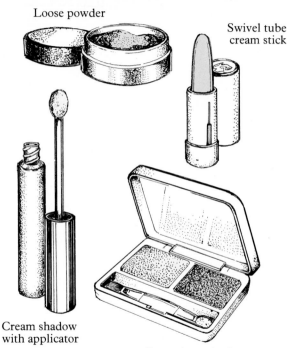

Loose powder

Swivel tube cream stick

Cream shadow with applicator

Pressed powder in compact

CREAM STICK APPLICATION

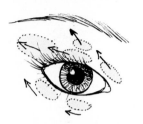

PRESSED POWDER APPLICATION

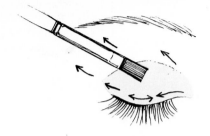

LIQUID CREAM

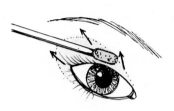

Stroke lightly around the eye area in small ovals, taking care not to apply too much. It is always easy to add more colour afterwards but difficult to remove any surplus. With the fingertip or a fine, clean brush, cotton swab or sponge-ended applicator, blend areas of colour until they merge softly. Always work from the inner eye out.

Using a fine, blunt-ended brush, gently apply colour to the lid. Start with your base colour, feathered lightly from the inside of the eye, and work up toward the brow bone, then outward. Apply deeper tones for added emphasis, using a clean brush, and blend well where colours meet to avoid hard and aging lines. Lightly brush over the colour closest to the lashes, working from the outside of the lid in. Always test colours on the back of the hand to see their intensity once applied.

LOOSE POWDERS
Use sparingly, picking up just the smallest amount on the brush. Always tap it on the back of your hand to remove excess powder, or it will end up on your cheekbone.

Liquid cream usually comes in a tube with a pointed, sponge-tipped applicator. As you remove the applicator, squeeze the surplus off the sponge tip by pressing on the side of the tube. Apply lightly around the eye, as shown, and smooth over with a cotton swab or clean brush, to even the texture. A heavy hand will make colour streak and cake.

Colouring in

Be adventurous with eye make-up—be bold, be daring. There is a dazzling array of colours to choose from and the effects you can create are virtually endless. Find the shades that work best for you by experimenting, then mix and match your own palette of toning colours or brave it with brilliant contrasts.

Take note ...
- Don't pick shades that match your eyes: they will not enhance their colour.
- Blue eyes light up with rich mahogany browns, deep coppers or smoky charcoals.
- Add highlighter to the brow bone, a pale, peachy shade by day and a cool ivory at night.

- Green eyes are stunning surrounded by rusty browns, gleaming coppers or hot apricots. Greys make green eyes go cold.
- Brown eyes grow soft and more intense with any shade of mauve.
- A tiny spot of pale highlighter at the center of the upper lid will open the eyes wide.

SMALL EYES

Soft and natural for day; use beige on the lid, mid-brown in the socket and darker brown outside. Use a white pencil inside the lower lid.

Make big eyes by clever blending and strengthen colour at top center of socket. Keep lids light and use a dark shade under lower lashes.

To extend eyes, sweep colour to the outside of the eye, to merge with darker shades below the lower lashes. Pencil inside the lower lid.

To make eyes smoulder, use jewel tones: light on and inside the lid, deeper across the brow bone and below the eye. Pencil inside the lower lid.

ALMOND EYES

By day, try several tones of one colour: pale on the lid and brow bone, mid-tone in the socket and a deeper shade smudged along the lashes.

For a fresh-faced look, brush the eyebrows up and use peach or pink on the brow bone, pastel over the lid. Darken the socket and under lashes.

Slant eyes mysteriously, with a mid-tone swept out over the outer lid. Highlight the brow bone from the center out and keep the socket light.

Go for exotic, iridescent shades at night. Use colour up to the eyebrow and charcoal at the outer corner of the top lid and under the lower lashes.

ROUND EYES

The soft, simple look needs a neutral shade over the lid, light brown in the socket and a fine outline of darker brown close to the lashes.

To change the eye shape, sweep dark colour all around the eye and out to the eyebrow. Sketch a mid-tone around the socket and line with kohl.

To emphasize the natural shape, keep the lid and brow bone light and use one tone darker in the socket. Colour below the eye and use eyeliner.

For striking effect, use a jewel colour drawn below the eyes and beyond. Keep lids and brow bone *au naturel* in grey or brown.

Adding depth

Depth and intensity, drama and expression come to the eyes through clever use of the definers. Eyeliners, pencils, kohls and mascaras in rich, darkly shaded colours emphasize the eyes, create new shapes and give the eyes a mysterious and exotic allure. The rules stay the same as for shadowing: practice makes perfect and hard lines should never be in evidence.

Take note ...
● Liquid eyeliners are a little difficult to use; try instead the cake type that is used with water and a fine brush; you will find it easier to control.
● Make sure that your eye pencils are soft and go on smoothly without dragging the skin.

● Experiment with coloured pencils, particularly the vibrant jewel tones; they can look sensational inside the lower lid. Have a white eye pencil on hand, it helps to widen the eyes.
● Pick sensible mascara colours; the deep, dark shades work best.

Lash luster
Use eyelash curlers gently, pressing the sections lightly together, without squeezing, to ensure a graceful curve. If your lashes are very long, curl them in two places, close to the roots and nearer the tips. Always apply mascara after curling and try to avoid that spiky black fringe around the eyes. Whenever you use a waterproof or water-resistant mascara, use a specially formulated remover at night. Regular cleansers are ineffective in this situation and can often irritate the eyes.

APPLICATION
Eyeliner
Add a drop of water to the cake of eyeliner and work your brush around until it holds. Test on the back of your hand to see what pressure should be applied. Unless you are a

Eye pencils
Pencils can be used in the same way as liner to define or extend the shape, but they give a much softer, more natural line. Keep them sharpened and ready for

Mascara
Most mascaras today come in a tube with a spiral brush applicator, but the good old-fashioned cake and brush varieties are still popular. The new-style, so-called "professional", mascaras

real artist, it is best to steady your elbow on a flat surface. Always work from the center of the eye to the outside corner and keep your line light and even. If you stop at the corner of the eyes, the effect will be round and wide-eyed; if you continue the line and sweep it up and out, a more exotic look can be achieved. Unless you want that stylized look, smudge edges afterwards with a cotton swab or fingertip to soften them.

use; a blunted or broken point can spoil the whole effect. Many make-up artists say that a medium-toned pencil is one of the most useful items in the cosmetic drawer, for it can line the lids and also shade the socket shape for extra emphasis. Black, charcoal and brown are best for defining, but the brights can be used for special effects, and white as a highlighter or eye opener.

have a curved spiral brush which makes for easy application. Coat both top and bottom of upper lashes, starting at the roots, working toward the tips and allowing each coat to dry before applying the next. Brush lashes well with a clean mascara brush or fine comb to keep them well separated. Take extra care if you use a mascara that contains tiny fibers to make lashes look thicker and longer and watch for flaking.

Finished eyes

Just as fashion changes from season to season, with exciting and different designs emerging to set future trends, so the big names in couture cosmetic houses regularly introduce a colourful crop of fresh and pretty shades to coordinate with the new looks. Once you have perfected the art of making eyes beautiful, you will also have confidence to make changes, adapting your make-up style to suit your mood, the occasion or the latest fashion look.

Ease for eyes
Your eyes express your every emotion; they also reveal signs of tension and tiredness. Soothe away redness and irritation by using eye drops, and refresh the eye area with cold-water compresses or tea bags soaked in water and gently squeezed out. The tissue surrounding the eye is fine and delicate, so avoid rubbing or pulling the skin. Never read in poor light if you can avoid it, it will strain the eyes and line your brow. If you develop any sort of eye infection, consult your doctor *immediately*. Most complaints can be sorted out quickly and easily but, if left, can cause great discomfort.

Glasses
Sunglasses are a necessity to protect the eyes against strong sunlight or glare from snow or water, but cheap or damaged lenses must be avoided. As a guide, C39 lenses are lightweight and very hard-wearing; photochromatics lighten or darken with the level of natural light; polarized lenses cut down reflected glare from flat surfaces and are ideal for sport. If you wear prescription glasses, have your eyes checked regularly in case you need a change in lens strength. Never borrow someone else's glasses. If you use contact lenses, opt for hypo-allergenic eye products to avoid possible irritants.

Enigmatic eyes
Sooty shades of black and grey merge with a hot, frosted pink and give eyes a look of magic and mystery. Kohl, worn inside the lower lid, adds a touch of the exotic.

Lipstick application

To apply lipstick perfectly, you need a steady hand, a fair bit of practice and the right tools. If you don't have the time to do it properly, don't do it at all. Opt for lip gloss instead.

Take note ...
- Moisturize your lips well at night and protect them from dryness and chapping in extreme temperatures by using an enriched lip salve.
- Test lipstick colours on the back of your hand to see how they affect your natural skin tones.
- Invest in good-quality, non-greasy lipsticks and keep them in a cool place, away from the sun. A drawer or make-up box are ideal.

- Always use a magnifying mirror and apply your lipstick in a good light.
- Steady your elbow on a solid surface.
- Unless you are planning to wear a natural lip gloss only, always powder lips first.
- Make sure your lips are smooth, dry and grease-free before you apply lipstick.
- Don't pile on the colour. It is easier to add than to remove lipstick.

ESSENTIAL EQUIPMENT

Narrow, flat-ended brush

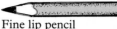
Fine lip pencil

Cream lipstick with applicator

Lipstick in swivel tube

The right tools are all essential. Whether you choose a conventional tube lipstick or a cream type with a sponge-tipped applicator, you will need a good lip brush and some finely sharpened lip pencils.

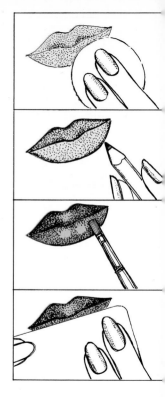

Prepare

When you apply your foundation, carry it over the entire lip area. Powder lips lightly with loose or pressed powder to create a perfect base for your lipstick. Remove any excess with a clean powder brush.

Outline

Use a sharp pencil in a shade close to that of your lipstick and, with a steady hand, lightly outline the lips. For the top lip, start at the center and work out toward the corner of the mouth. For the lower lip, work from side to side.

Colour in

Stroke your brush on the lipstick to collect colour and apply it to the top lip, starting at the center and working outward. If using a cream type, smooth over with a lip brush after application.

Blotting

Fold a clean tissue in half and place it between your lips. Press lips lightly together to remove excess lipstick and to help seal the remainder so that it stays on your lips and not on every glass and cup you use.

SHAPE UP

Thin lips are easily corrected by taking the pencil outside the natural lip line. Work slowly and steadily before you fill in with colour. Add a highlight of frosting to the upper lip.

Overfull lips can be made to look smaller if you pencil the outline just inside the natural shape and use medium-toned lipstick colours. Stay away from the extremes, dark and light, and avoid shimmer.

Crooked lips need not be cursed. Study the fault well and, with a bit of practice, you should be able to adjust your lips perfectly by balancing the pencil outline above or below the natural shape.

Shapeless lips can be turned into the perfect cupid's bow if you never neglect to powder well first. Outline the most flattering shape, emphasizing a firm center to the top lip and adding fullness to the lower.

35

The perfect mouth

Lipsticks today come in a vast range of shades, from the palest of pastels to the brightest of bolds; from soft, subtle pinks and peaches to burnished browns and rich, ruby reds. Choose your colours with care and remember that the mouth should never take over the face nor detract from the eyes. Lipsticks of a similar tone to your blusher will create a soft and glowing look; a dramatic contrast can be devastating after dark but disastrous from nine to five. Experiment with a whole wardrobe of colours—clear, vivid brights and gleaming shimmer-shades.

THE COLOUR GROUPS

Reds
Bold and brilliant, from the strong, sensuous scarlets to the deepest gleaming crimson.

Oranges
Terrific with a tan, but mousy browns should avoid vivid and white- or yellow-based shades.

Burgundies
Rich, intense and striking on dark brunettes. Colours range from ruby red to deep claret.

Pinks
Flattering, from the filmy pales through the rose tones to the rich, ripe raspberries.

Browns
Keep to the peach, apricot and caramel shades. Avoid the flat, deep earth-tones.

Mauves
Always different and often delightful, go for those with a generous hint of pink.

FINDING THE RIGHT COLOUR

A beautifully coloured, perfectly painted mouth completes any look; the wrong shade or hurried application can spell disaster. Whatever fashion dictates, never wear a colour you don't feel quite right in, and always remember to change your lipstick shade with your clothes.

Clear, strong lipstick colours look marvellous with dark, single-coloured clothes; mid-tones work well with pale shades and soft, fluid fabrics.

If you are wearing a bright, multi-coloured print, choose a lipstick to pick out, or tone with, one of the shades in the print. Lip colours look different on every face and must always

complement natural skin tones. Brunettes, of all shades, must avoid yellow-based colours if their skin is slightly sallow. Pale mousy

browns should forget about strong reds, mauves and oranges. Medium to dark brunettes, especially those lucky enough to

have a pale creamy complexion, can go to town with all the clear, bright shades such as strong, hot pinks, sharp poppy reds and clean pinky mauves.

Dark earth-tones can look draining on most brunettes, but pink-coppers and peaches show up a treat. If your hair is really dark, always wear lipstick to bring life and colour to the face. Lighter hair colourings can look wonderful in a softly tinted lip gloss in the daylight.

Just as you would change your lipstick colour to make a transition from a day to a night look, remember to change with the seasons. Try extremes of the same shade; the paler, softer version in summer; richer tones from autumn on.

Colour chart

Choosing the best and prettiest make-up colours is easy; picking the ones which work with each other requires a little precision matching. As a rule, don't mix strong contrasts and always add warmth to pale pastels. Use darker eye colours to shadow and shape, lighter shades to highlight and lipsticks and blushers to complement the eyes.

YOUR COLOUR KALEIDOSCOPE
FOR CHEEKS, EYES, LIPS

Mousy brown hair	Blushers	Eye shadows
Blue eyes	Pink	Mushroom, clove slate-grey, pink
Green eyes	Peach	Wine, grape, salmon pink, apricot
Grey eyes	Rose-pink	Sapphire, eggshell midnight, copper
Brown eyes	Deep peach	Lavender, mulberry, lilac
Medium brown hair		
Blue eyes	True rose	Heather, charcoal copper, pink-rust
Green eyes	Coral	Lilac, orchid-pink grey-brown, mauve
Grey eyes	Rich rose	Heather, grey-blue charcoal, black
Brown eyes	Paprika	Damson, violet, aubergine, black

sticks
e raspberry, k-mauve, pink
ep apricot, non, peach
sty rose, k pink, copper
t cherry, p peach, apricot

k rose, ice-pink, ch-pink
al, tangerine, ht pink-mauve
rry, deep rose, ht pink
nge-gold, ve-pink, copper

Dark brown hair	Blushers	Eye shadows	Lipsticks
Blue eyes	Dusty pink	Midnight, claret, rose, turquoise	Deep raspberry, pink-mauve, poppy
Green eyes	Tawny pink	Sapphire, emerald, mahogany, copper	Rose, raspberry, chestnut
Grey eyes	Rich rose	Aubergine, damson, black, pink-pearl	Cerise, deep red, dusty rose
Brown eyes	Copper	Pineapple, brown, violet, blue-black	Burnt orange, deep copper, raspberry
Brown, going grey			
Blue eyes	Soft pink	Cornflower, slate, rust, deep rose	Pink, strong rose, pale copper-pink
Green eyes	Salmon	Eau-de-nil, mushroom, lavender	Coral, deep salmon, pale cherry
Grey eyes	Rose pink	Heather, charcoal, slate, pale rose	Pink, dusty rose, mulberry
Brown eyes	Deep apricot	Brown, sand, honey, mauve	Clear red, rust, pink-brown

Dress sense

Trend-setting clothes, which are outlandish in design and gimmicky in detail, may look great in a magazine or on the catwalk at a fashion show. However, few of us have either the beanpole figure or the sort of lifestyle that will allow us to dress successfully in the crazy-coloured, strange-shaped offerings from today's more way-out designers. Real style is quite different; it is not so much about the clothes you wear as the way you wear them. Clever dressers use flair and imagination to accessorize a simple, well-cut garment and turn it into something chic, stunning and highly individual.

In the stores
Take advantage of the seasonal sales to buy special investments such as classically cut silk shirts and simply styled cashmere sweaters. The bright, fashion high-fliers may be tempting, but if they are in the sale, they are out of date. Before you buy anything, try it on first; what looks good in a window or on a hanger may not look so good on a real person! Don't buy clothes one size too small and convince yourself that you will diet into them. Diet first, then go on a spending spree. Before investing in a pair of pants, check your back view in a mirror and ensure the lines are smooth and slimming.

Your wardrobe
A colour theme of three main shades is the best basis for any wardrobe. That way, you can mix and match, tone and contrast and create new styles from old. For a touch of high-fashion colour, introduce exciting accessories—belts, scarves and jewelry. Don't, however, buy a bag or a pair of shoes to wear with just one outfit, you will almost certainly regret it later. Enjoy your wardrobe and ignore what the fashion pundits dictate. If you like your skirts long, wear them that way. If the mini is your style, show your knees. But, one word of warning, avoid prints with strong colour contrast or too large a design. They can swamp you and detract from your face.

COLOUR SCHEMES

The colours that suit brunettes best depend on their hair colouring. Mousy brown looks best in clear colours, but drab in earthy tones. Those with medium- to light-brown hair should go for the rich, strong shades of blue, green and pink, and the classical pales—vanilla, ivory and lavender. Avoid brown- or yellow-tinged colours; biscuit, mustard and rusty tans lack the warmth to light up the face; dark shades of navy, charcoal and chocolate are equally draining. Bright pillar-box red, brilliant electric blue, rich greens and strong yellows look superb on dark brunettes with warm skin tones. Choose shades that bring out the colour of your eyes.

Vibrant shades

Rich, strong shades

Classical pales

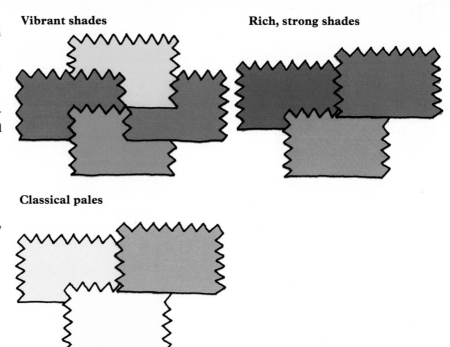

The facial massage

Any form of massage is wonderfully relaxing and helps ease away tension in the muscles while it soothes, smooths and revives the skin. Facial massage has the added benefit of being a beauty treatment in its own right—the movements stimulate blood circulation and help repair any damage to the skin, leaving it soft, tingling and fresh.

Take note ...
• Give yourself a facial massage at least once or twice a month. It is important that you relax and enjoy the total experience—the calmer you feel, the better the results will be. Your massage should last 10 to 15 minutes; any longer would be too tiring.

• Always use a cream or oil suited to your skin type. An oil-free medicated cream is best by far for those with greasy skin; a few drops of warm almond oil is a treat for dry skins.
• Young skin needs only a light moisturizing lotion, while more mature skins will benefit from an enriched cream.

After the massage
When you have completed your home massage, remove every trace of cream or lotion, then cleanse thoroughly in the usual way. After applying the toner for your skin type, let the face rest, then wait a while before applying make-up. Better still, do your massage in the evening before going to bed, but never forget the final cleanse, tone and nourish routine, to ensure healthy, well-balanced skin.

MASSAGE METHOD

1 Tie hair back off the face.
2 Smooth your moisturizer, oil or cream over the face and neck.
3 With hands facing inward, start at the base of the neck and run fingers lightly up over the face, one hand following the other to the center.

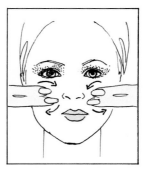

4 Using your first and second fingers only, tap lightly all over the face.
5 With the thumb and first finger, gently knead the chin, around the mouth and the fleshy part of the cheeks. Don't pull or pinch at the skin, but keep the movements firm, even and steady.

6 Soothe and smooth the forehead by "ironing" over fine lines. Hold the skin firm between the first and second fingers on one hand, then use the first finger of the other hand to massage the skin in an in-and-out movement. Repeat over each area of the forehead.

7 Again using your first two fingers, run them over the cheeks in small, circular movements, always in the direction of the nose.

8 Now concentrate on the eye area. With the fourth finger of each hand, lightly smooth over the brow bone to the outside of the eye, then bring the fingers below the eyes and back to the center. With the little finger, gently press around the outside of the eye, especially where fine lines are present, and release immediately. Rotate fingertips on temples to ease any tension.
9 Repeat the first massage movement again, close your eyes, and relax for a few minutes.

43

The look

The twenties are one of the great periods in life—exhilarating, exciting, stimulating and fun. It is a time when everything is new, different and waiting to be discovered, a time when you develop the self-assurance and confidence to make the most of your new-found freedom and the best of your great young looks. You can be fresh-faced and natural one day, a cool, sophisticated dazzler the next—the choice is yours and you are at just the right age to change your look as often as you change your mind.

Take note ...
● Eat well and eat sensibly. Don't go on crazy diets; don't starve yourself and then go on an eating binge; don't ever skip breakfast.

● Make sure you get enough sleep and outdoor exercise.
● Keep your hair in good condition, with a weekly treatment, particularly if you colour and curl it.

Skin care
It is worth keeping your skin in terrific shape, since the routine you adopt now will keep you looking good in the years ahead. If you have greasy skin, avoid the foods that will aggravate the condition. Life without a daily dose of chips and chocolate is still okay. Severe spot sufferers should consult their doctors and use products designed specifically to combat the problem.

Corkscrew curls, big brown eyes and a sprinkling of freckles ar delightful left *au nature* But see what a differenc the right make-up can achieve. Stylishly casua good looks by day are created with a delicious fresh combination of so pinks and blue-greys. A night, cover-girl chic emerges from smoky shades of charcoal, heather and peach-pear

Getting it together

It takes a lot of experimenting to perfect your look. Play around with colour and paint the prettiest images possible—you will never know if violet eye shadow is sheer delight or absolute disaster until you try it. By day, go for a healthy glow; use tinted moisturizer, a fluffing of blusher and a slicking of lip gloss. At night, go wild; go way-out; go totally over the top, in bright, vibrant colours and ritzy shimmer-shades.

Take note ...
● Choose a foundation with light coverage; at your age you should not need anything heavier.
● A strong, bold make-up calls for clever use of eye, cheek and lip shades. A slapped-on riot of colour looks just that.

● Try the unexpected; surprise combinations—lavender with apple-green, pink with yellow, peach with grey—look amazing on the eyes.
● However late at night, don't go to bed without first removing every last scrap of your make-up.

DAYTIME

Foundation
A warm, toasted-beige liquid cream foundation, with the lightest, faintest coverage to let the natural glow of the skin show through. As an alternative, try a deeper, honey-toned moisturizer for a fresh, outdoor look.

Blusher
A pretty rose-pink, fluffed over the cheeks and blended out toward the ears and temples.

Powder
A light dusting of translucent, loose face powder, to keep the face looking smooth and shine-free.

Hair
Well conditioned, and brushed off the face in a casual, tossed-about style.

Eyebrows
Naturally dark and wonderfully thick—a bonus point on young brunettes—lightly powdered and brushed into shape.

Lips
Outlined in a brownish pink, filled in with a creamy, dusty-rose lipstick, slicked over with lip gloss.

Eyes

Coloured to bring out the sparkle, a delicious mixture of grey, blue and pink has been used. The palest of the blue-greys is brushed over the lids and swept up and out at the corners of the eyes. A deeper, heather-grey is applied to the socket line and, above this, a soft pink-pearl. The brow bone is highlighted in an ivory-pink, which is echoed on the inner corner of the lids, blending over the grey to the center of the eyes. Definition comes with the finest line of charcoal grey, whisked close to the top and bottom lashes and smudged slightly. Lashes are curled and two coats of creamy black mascara are added.

EVENING

From "girl next door" to elegant eye-catcher: the foundation is warmer, in honey gold; the blusher sweeter, in spicy rose. Go for dramatically dark eyes, blending stronger shades of grey and blue with sooty black and charcoal. Complete with frosted peach on the brow bone and raspberry cream on the lips.

A style for you

Chances are, by the mid-thirties, a woman has come to know herself, to understand her looks and to have developed her own unique style. She will have noticed several changes, too, that have brought a maturity to her looks: the fine lines etched around the eyes, forehead and mouth; a less silky complexion; the first few grey hairs. But be she a busy career woman working to a hectic schedule, or a housewife and mother involved in family duties, she recognizes the need to look and feel great at all times. With practice and know-how, carefully selected colour cosmetics and skilful application, she can easily create an image that is coolly sophisticated and wonderfully feminine.

Skin care

Look after your skin as never before and always be disciplined in your skin care regime. Always make sure your skin is well protected. Use a moisturizer every day, a cream at night and high-protection-factor products when you are out in the sun. Remember, nothing accelerates the skin's aging process as quickly as prolonged exposure to the sun. Now is the time to invest in specialized products such as enriched creams for the eye area and the throat. Get your eating habits in order. Lots of fresh vegetables and fruit and virtually no fried or fatty foods will keep you slim and trim and ensure a healthy, glowing complexion.

Take a pretty brunette in her early thirties. Her skin is smooth and clear, thanks to a regular beauty routine, and her shoulder-length hair is cut in long layers so that a variety of styles is possible. By day she uses soft, warm make-up colours to bring a gentle glow. At night, a combination of violet, grey and black adds depth and drama to the eyes.

Applying the image

All the tricks of the trade can be applied to changing an image. Pick foundations that are softly flattering and shadows that bring out the true colour of your eyes. Always wear blusher and lipstick to keep your face warm, alive and glowing. By night, be daring with colour—brunettes are the lucky ones who can choose anything, from an aqua-tinted palette of rainbow pastels to a riot of rich, vibrant jewel shades.

Take note ...
● If your hair is greying, try a cover-up rinse or a semi-permanent tint.
● Skin tones and textures change over the years. Now may be the time for you to look at different types of foundation; shades with a touch more warmth could make a beautiful difference.

● Light brunettes should move toward a soft and subtle look by day, using warm shades to add colour and glow.
● Medium to dark brunettes, who have the natural colouring to take the brighter shades, must always avoid an over-painted look.

DAYTIME
Foundation
A liquid cream foundation in a beige-gold shade, with a lighter-coloured cream concealer, well blended beneath the eyes to hide shadows and fine lines.

Powder
Matt, translucent powder is pressed over the face, and the surplus removed with a clean powder brush.

Blusher
A soft, corally apricot is applied in a small semicircle, right on the point of the cheekbone, and fluffed on to the brow bone to give a healthy glow.

Hair
Sleekly sophisticated, pulled back into an off-the-face style, with a few soft waves at the front.

Eyebrows
Well defined to frame the eyes, the eyebrows have been shaped with a finely pointed light-brown eye pencil. It is applied in tiny strokes, following the natural line, then brushed in the direction of hair growth with a clean mascara brush.

Eyes

To keep the look strong but muted and to bring out the colour of the eyes, a soft sand shadow is applied over the whole lid. Depth is added with a rich brown shadow, used along the socket line and swept slightly up and out, then taken below the lower lashes. The eyes are defined with dark-brown liquid liner, applied with a fine brush and then gently smudged with a cotton swab. Lashes are curled and mascara'd in black.

Lips

The outline has been drawn in with a fine coral-brown pencil, and any faults corrected. The lipstick, a rich, but see-through, coral is applied with a lip brush and blended well into the outline.

EVENING
For a coolly sophisticated look, pick an ivory-toned foundation. Set your make-up with matt, translucent powder and fluff on warm, peachy blusher. Try violet over the eyelids and a sweep of damson in the sockets. Surround the eyes with liner and use three coats of mascara on the top lashes only. Bring out the vibrant eye colours with pale apricot lipstick.

A new you

Come the forties, your lifestyle goes through a change yet again. As career and family pressures ease, you suddenly discover you have more time to relax and enjoy life, time to devote to new or neglected interests. Invest some of that well-earned time in yourself and in your looks. By now your skin will be showing signs of the passing years, having lost its youthful bloom and elasticity. It may be drier than ever before because, with the approach of the menopause, the oil-producing sebaceous glands become smaller and less active. As facial lines deepen and skin tones alter, it is important to appraise your make-up style and to adapt it to suit your new maturity.

Skin care
Be alert to any changes in your skin; increased dryness and flaking can be counteracted by richer creams and moisturizers. Also watch the danger zones, the tell-tale areas that give away age, such as throat and neck. Treat them as part of your face and lavish enriched creams on them to keep them smooth, soft and well protected.
Remember that bad posture encourages wrinkling on the neck, so stand up straight. Don't even contemplate crash diets, a sudden weight loss makes mature skin look crepey and loose. It is wiser to cut down on fatty foods and sugar instead. Finally, keep your face out of the sun or use a block-out cream.

A rich, burnished-brown semi-permanent tint covers all traces of grey, and regular conditioning adds body and shine to extra-long hair. The ideal day make-up is soft, subtle and elegant, but by night, clever use of colour brings a bloom to the cheeks, a sparkle to the eyes and a wonderful, all-over feminine glow.

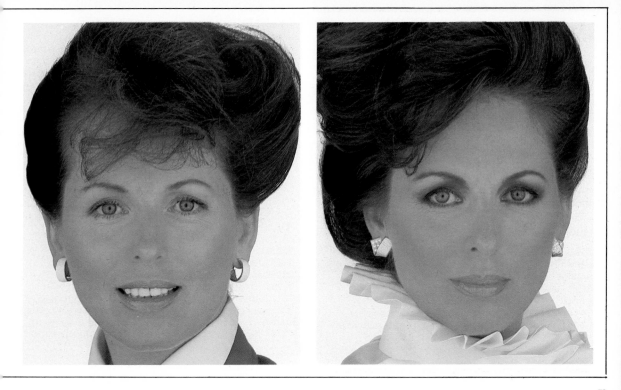

Adapting your look

As your image matures, it is time to take a fresh approach to make-up. Foundations that worked well for you in the past may now be too heavy in texture and colour, serving only to accentuate lines around the eyes, mouth and forehead. Blushers that once brought a glow to your cheeks could well be too bright or lacking in subtlety. Try to keep your look light, natural and pretty—an excess of make-up looks harsh and artificial, while strong eye and lip colours drain the face and add unnecessary years.

Take note ...
● Always use a good moisturizer or hydrating lotion under foundation.
● Switch to a light-coverage foundation and always blend it well on wrinkled areas.

● Use the minimum of powder and choose soft, pretty eyeshadows—always matt.
● Pick warm, clear colours for blushers; avoid bright, mauve or brown tones.

DAYTIME
Foundation
A warm, golden-beige, light liquid foundation, blended over the face and neck, evens the skin tones and enhances the complexion. A cream-beige concealer stick is used to hide dark shadows beneath the eyes and to disguise tiny red veins on the nose.

Blusher
A warm peach, with just a hint of pink, is fluffed over the cheeks to emphasize the beautiful bone structure and is swept up to the temples for extra glow.

Hair
Off the face and smoothed into a simple back knot, with height and front curl to balance the face shape and soften the outline.

Eyebrows
Fine and feathered, shaped to a gently curving arch, well brushed and lightly defined with tiny strokes of grey-brown eye pencil.

Powder
The lightest dusting of loose, translucent powder is whisked over the face, avoiding the wrinkle-prone area just below the eyes.

Eyes

Softly and subtly shaded, in barely visible tones of peach, sand and grey, carefully blended until they merge. A fine line of grey liquid eyeliner is smudged close to the base of the upper lashes to give definition to the natural eye shape. It is repeated beneath the lower lashes, from the center to the outside of the eyes. Two coats of charcoal-grey mascara are applied, and the lashes are then brushed through to keep them well separated.

Lips

Powdered well to form a base for lipstick and outlined lightly with a pinky-brown pencil. Lips are filled in with a warm, tawny-rose shade and blotted well to remove the excess.

EVENING

For good, old-fashioned glamour, play up the eyes. To emphasize the sockets, use rich, deep greys, swept out at the sides to lengthen the eyes; use terracotta above to bring out their blue. Frame them with charcoal liner and black mascara. Pale peach highlights the brow bone. The blusher is a true coral-pink, the lipstick a warm, rich rose.

Into the fifties

Around the mid-fifties, everything in the body starts to slow down. You tire easily, become susceptible to aches and pains in the back and joints and to a weakening in the muscles. The body's ability to produce estrogen, the valuable female hormone that helps keep your skin and hair young and healthy, decreases with the menopause. Although hormone replacement treatment can help redress the balance, you must remember that there are no magical potions to prevent the aging process. However, a lifetime of regular and sensible skin care, good eating habits and shelter from the sun will all help slow down the process, and there is no reason why a women over fifty should not be every bit as attractive as she was ten years earlier.

Skin care
Your skin is drier and more delicate than ever before, so use mild skin care products with softeners added. Once or twice a month, use a face mask, to tighten the skin and brighten the complexion. Eat lots of fresh fruit, raw vegetables and fish, and if your diet is lacking, supplement it with vitamin pills or brewer's yeast. Exercise is all-important for you now. A regular walk will help keep you slim, trim and healthy and improve the circulation; face and neck exercises will ease away tension and get the muscles working.

A look of elegance and understated chic can easily be achieved from the basic ingredients; clear, superbly cared-for skin and expertly cut, coloured and conditioned hair. Skilful use of colour cosmetics makes for striking good looks.

Setting a style

Your face really needs colour now because the skin looks paler and more delicate than ever before. The right, carefully selected shades can bring a marvellous new radiance to your complexion and a warm softness to your eyes. Badly chosen colours, which are too strong or tinged with blue or yellow, dull the skin and deaden the sparkle, as do over-bright or boldly patterned clothes.

Take note ...
- Review your foundation colour every few years. As skin tones lighten, you may well need a softer shade.
- Keep blusher high on the cheekbones to avoid a painted look.
- Always wear lipstick.

- Keep your eye colours soft and warm, the cooler tones of shadow will make your eyes look cold.
- Always outline the lips with a pencil before applying lipstick. As you get older, natural lines fade and need good reshaping.

DAYTIME
Foundation
After applying a fine film of non-greasy moisturizer, a light, honey-cream foundation is smoothed over the face and neck for an even glow. Dark shadows and small blemishes are concealed with a slightly lighter foundation. Use a dampened sponge to blend, especially around the hair-line.

Blusher
Warm, peach-pink tones are swept high on the cheekbones and to the hair-line for a soft glow.

Powder
A fine, translucent powder is pressed lightly over the face, and the surplus removed with a soft brush. Avoid using powder where the skin is lined, or it will cake in the creases.

Hair
Naturally streaked with grey, silver and white, an attractive pepper and salt effect is created. Keep the style easy to manage so that you can change it to suit the occasion.

Eyebrows
Sparser now than before, they need good shaping and defining in mid-brown eye pencil. Brush them afterwards with a clean mascara brush to keep the lines smooth and soft.

Lips
Carry foundation over the lips, powder well and remove any surplus powder before lightly outlining them with a soft, but true, pink moisturizing lipstick.

Eyes

Just the barest hint of colour is all that is necessary for day. Choose soft shades such as the pastel grey-blue shown here. Keep colour light over the lids; dark shadows in the socket line emphasize crepey skin and can sink eyes too deeply to be attractive. The finest line of darker grey near the base of the upper lashes gives all the definition needed, but it stops at the outer corner of the eye to keep the shape natural. Two coats of brownish-black mascara add a soft fringe of colour to the eyes.

EVENING
Stay with the same foundation. Warm the cheeks with a richer, tawny-rose blusher, and bring the eyes to life with a carefully blended combination of cinnamon and grey, with soft peach-pink worn as a highlighter on the brow bone. A faint suggestion of grey just below the lower lashes will define the eyes and contour their shape.

Year-round good looks

Just as fashion and lifestyle change from summer to winter, so should the style and colouring of your make-up. In the warm, mid-year months, when the strong, bright light of the sun exposes every detail of the face, your look should be kept fresh, cool and deliberately natural. As the weather gets colder and summery pastel clothes give way to the darker, richer colours, heavier fabrics and layered dressing, the skin is at its palest and needs added warmth to make it glow.

Summer secrets
Go easy with foundation or, better still, use a tan-tinted moisturizer during the day—natural sunlight has a nasty habit of turning a made-up face into a clownish mask.

Change your make-up and keep it light. Pick pale, flower-fresh pastels, muted coppers and soft browns. Put away the stronger shades of blusher and opt for peach rather than pink.

In the sun

If your skin is dry, use an oil-based sun screen and a rich moisturizer. Don't let your lips dry out; protect them well with a special sun screen. Remember that intense sunlight and prolonged sunbathing is damaging to all skin types, even those that tan easily and evenly. Always use a suntan preparation with the correct protection-factor for your skin type and reapply it frequently, especially after swimming. If you have sensitive skin, try to stay in the shade and use a sun block-out cream.

Winter skin care

Constantly protect skin against the harsh, drying effects of cold weather, wind and central heating. Dry and sensitive skins suffer particularly at this time of year, so always moisturize well.

Autumn overhaul

At the end of the summer, get your hair into peak condition. You will need regular treatments to replace all that the sun has taken out and to regain a healthy, shimmering shine.

Warm winter looks

Artificial light affects the tone of your cosmetics, so always double-check colours to make sure they suit your complexion in both natural and electric light. If you are very pale, don't try to give yourself colour by using a dark foundation; the result will be hard and unnatural. Use lots of blusher instead, to warm the face and create a beautiful soft glow. This is the time for strong eye colours. Try the richer jewel tones, the burnished brights and the sooty shades of black, brown and grey for emphasis.

Magical tips

Virtually everyone has her own favourite beauty tip: one that has been passed down from mother to daughter, borrowed from a friend or gleaned from the glossy magazines. These range from simple, but effective, skin and hair care hints to methods of creating superb optical illusions through unusual use of colour and its stylized application. Here are some of the best tips to start off your own collection.

With just one brown eye pencil you can conjure up a whole look. Smudge a shadow in the socket, outline the eyes, faintly etch around the lids.

A tiny dot of red pencil at the inner corner of the eyes makes them look larger, more dreamy.

Walk away with the glittering prizes—brush just a gleam of gold on the eyebrows, a touch of shimmery iridescent colour on the center of the lips. You will create a sensation if you add frosted highlights to your hair. Buy the spray-on, brush-out in gold or silver.

To keep eyebrows natural-looking, try using two shades of pencil, one a touch lighter than the other.

Sharpen eyebrow pencils with a blade and create two flat surfaces. The finely chiselled end will make for easy application.

If your skin is excessively greasy and you find oil-free foundations difficult to apply, try a liquid cream type and add just a few drops of astringent, mixing them together in the palm of your hand.

A mixture of rosewater and witch hazel makes a refreshing toner.

Don't slip up by throwing away banana skins. The inside, wiped over spots, helps clear them quickly and naturally.

Drink a couple of pints of water a day—it is a great purifier for your insides and your complexion will show the benefits too.

When you buy cosmetic sponges, cut them in wedges—like slices of cake—the side panels will be the right size and shape for contouring.

Never waste face creams by removing the excess from your hands with a tissue; rub them in, not off, and your hands will stay smooth and soft.

Use pure lemon juice to remove stains and ingrained dirt from the fingers and around the nail area.

Don't attempt to bleach facial hair at home, the results are rarely successful and you could mark your skin. Consult a professional for advice.

Don't use deodorants if you are planning to sunbathe.

When travelling, transfer cleansers and toners to small-size plastic bottles, to save packing space and weighty luggage and to avoid the risk of broken glass.

Another travelling tip: to keep make-up brushes in good order, bundle them together in an elastic band, wrap the tips in tissue and pack them in a plastic bag. Store sponges in plastic, too, to stop them drying out.

If your complexion has a lot of red pigment, don't wear blue-pinks, mauves and fuchsia colours next to the face.

Remember that pale colours always flatter most. You can't go wrong with white, cream, ivory or buttermilk.

If you change your hair-style or your hair colour, your make-up will also probably need a change.

When you give yourself a pedicure, put a cotton ball between your toes to stop polish smudging.

Use hair-setting mousse to give shape and fullness to your cut; it is especially good in a sun-sand-sea situation, since it protects the hair too.